2017

EDITION ANANDA

ISBN-10: 1537383280
ISBN-13: 978-1537383286

2017

January	February	March	April	May	June
1 Su New Year's Day	1 We	1 We	1 Sa	1 Mo	1 Th
2 Mo	2 Th	2 Th	2 Su	2 Tu	2 Fr
3 Tu	3 Fr	3 Fr	3 Mo	3 We	3 Sa
4 We	4 Sa	4 Sa	4 Tu	4 Th	4 Su
5 Th	5 Su	5 Su	5 We	5 Fr	5 Mo
6 Fr	6 Mo	6 Mo	6 Th	6 Sa	6 Tu
7 Sa	7 Tu	7 Tu	7 Fr	7 So	7 We
8 Su	8 We	8 We	8 Sa	8 Mo	8 Th
9 Mo	9 Th	9 Th	9 Su	9 Tu	9 Fr
10 Tu	10 Fr	10 Fr	10 Mo	10 We	10 Sa
11 We	11 Sa	11 Sa	11 Tu	11 Th	11 Su
12 Th	12 Su	12 Su	12 We	12 Fr	12 Mo
13 Fr	13 Mo	13 Mo	13 Th	13 Sa	13 Tu
14 Sa	14 Tu	14 Tu	14 Fr	14 Su	14 We
15 Su	15 We	15 We	15 Sa	15 Mo	15 Th
16 Mo Martin L. King Day	16 Th	16 Th	16 Su	16 Tu	16 Fr
17 Tu	17 Fr	17 Fr	17 Mo	17 We	17 Sa
18 We	18 Sa	18 Sa	18 Tu	18 Th	18 Su
19 Th	19 Su	19 Su	19 We	19 Fr	19 Mo
20 Fr	20 Mo Presidents' Day	20 Mo	20 Th	20 Sa	20 Tu
21 Sa	21 Tu	21 Tu	21 Fr	21 Su	21 We
22 Su	22 We	22 We	22 Sa	22 Mo	22 Th
23 Mo	23 Th	23 Th	23 Su	23 Tu	23 Fr
24 Tu	24 Fr	24 Fr	24 Mo	24 We	24 Sa
25 We	25 Sa	25 Sa	25 Tu	25 Th	25 Su
26 Th	26 Su	26 Su	26 We	26 Fr	26 Mo
27 Fr	27 Mo	27 Mo	27 Th	27 Sa	27 Tu
28 Sa	28 Tu	28 Tu	28 Fr	28 Su	28 We
29 Su		29 We	29 Sa	29 Mo Memorial Day	29 Th
30 Mo		30 Th	30 Su	30 Tu	30 Fr
31 Tu		31 Fr		31 We	

Data provided 'as is' without warranty

2017

July	August	September	October	November	December
1 Sa	1 Tu	1 Fr	1 Su	1 We	1 Fr
2 Su	2 We	2 Sa	2 Mo	2 Th	2 Sa
3 Mo	3 Th	3 Su	3 Tu	3 Fr	3 Su
4 Tu Independence Day	4 Fr	4 Mo Labor Day	4 We	4 Sa	4 Mo
5 We	5 Sa	5 Tu	5 Th	5 Su	5 Tu
6 Th	6 Su	6 We	6 Fr	6 Mo	6 We
7 Fr	7 Mo	7 Th	7 Sa	7 Tu	7 Th
8 Sa	8 Tu	8 Fr	8 Su	8 We	8 Fr
9 Su	9 We	9 Sa	9 Mo Columbus Day	9 Th	9 Sa
10 Mo	10 Th	10 Su	10 Tu	10 Fr Veterans Day	10 Su
11 Tu	11 Fr	11 Mo	11 We	11 Sa	11 Mo
12 We	12 Sa	12 Tu	12 Th	12 Su	12 Tu
13 Th	13 Su	13 We	13 Fr	13 Mo	13 We
14 Fr	14 Mo	14 Th	14 Sa	14 Th	14 Th
15 Sa	15 Tu	15 Fr	15 Su	15 We	15 Fr
16 Su	16 We	16 Sa	16 Mo	16 Th	16 Sa
17 Mo	17 Th	17 Su	17 Tu	17 Fr	17 Su
18 Tu	18 Fr	18 Mo	18 We	18 Sa	18 Mo
19 We	19 Sa	19 Tu	19 Th	19 Su	19 Tu
20 Th	20 Su	20 We	20 Fr	20 Mo	20 We
21 Fr	21 Mo	21 Th	21 Sa	21 Tu	21 Th
22 Sa	22 Tu	22 Fr	22 Su	22 We	22 Fr
23 Su	23 We	23 Sa	23 Mo	23 Th Thanksgiving Day	23 Sa
24 Mo	24 Th	24 Su	24 Tu	24 Fr	24 Su
25 Tu	25 Fr	25 Mo	25 We	25 Sa	25 Mo Christmas Day
26 We	26 Sa	26 Tu	26 Th	26 Su	26 Tu Christmas Day
27 Th	27 Su	27 We	27 Fr	27 Mo	27 We
28 Fr	28 Mo	28 Th	28 Sa	28 Tu	28 Th
29 Sa	29 Tu	29 Fr	29 Su	29 We	29 Fr
30 Su	30 We	30 Sa	30 Mo	30 Th	30 Sa
31 Mo	31 Th		31 Tu		31 Su

Data provided 'as is' without warranty

December 2016

26 Monday

27 Tuesday

28 Wednesday

Data provided 'as is' without warranty

January 2017

29 Thursday

30 Friday

31 Saturday

01 Sunday **New Year's Day**

Data provided 'as is' without warranty

02 Monday
03 Tuesday
04 Wednesday

Data provided 'as is' without warranty

January 2017

05 Thursday

06 Friday

07 Saturday

08 Sunday

Data provided 'as is' without warranty

09 Monday

10 Tuesday

11 Wednesday

January 2017

12 Thursday

13 Friday Lee Jackson Day

14 Saturday

15 Sunday

Data provided 'as is' without warranty

16 Monday **Martin L. King Day**

Idaho Human Rights Day

Robert E Lee's Birthday
(Alabama, Arkansas,Mississippi)

17 Tuesday

18 Wednesday

Data provided 'as is' without warranty

January 2017

19 Thursday

Robert E Lee's Birthday
(Florida)

20 Friday

21 Saturday

22 Sunday

Data provided 'as is' without warranty

23 Monday

24 Tuesday

25 Wednesday

January 2017

26 Thursday

27 Friday

28 Saturday

29 Sunday Kansas Day

30 Monday

31 Tuesday

01 Wednesday

Data provided 'as is' without warranty

February 2017

02 Thursday

03 Friday

04 Saturday Rosa Parks Day

05 Sunday

Data provided 'as is' without warranty

06 Monday

07 Tuesday

08 Wednesday

February 2017

09 Thursday

10 Friday

11 Saturday

12 Sunday — Lincoln's Birthday

Data provided 'as is' without warranty

13 Monday

14 Tuesday

15 Wednesday Susan B Anthony's Birthday

Data provided 'as is' without warranty

February 2017

16 Thursday

17 Friday

18 Saturday

19 Sunday

Data provided 'as is' without warranty

20 Monday

Presidents Day
Washington's Birthday

21 Tuesday

22 Wednesday

Data provided 'as is' without warranty

February 2017

23 Thursday

24 Friday

25 Saturday

26 Sunday

Data provided 'as is' without warranty

27 Monday

28 Tuesday

01 Wednesday

Data provided 'as is' without warranty

March 2017

02 Thursday Texas,Independence Day

03 Friday

04 Saturday

05 Sunday

Data provided 'as is' without warranty

06 Monday Casimir Pulaski Day

07 Tuesday Town Meeting Day Vermont

08 Wednesday

Data provided 'as is' without warranty

March 2017

09 Thursday

10 Friday

11 Saturday

12 Sunday

Data provided 'as is' without warranty

13 Monday

14 Tuesday

15 Wednesday

Data provided 'as is' without warranty

March 2017

16 Thursday

17 Friday Evacuation Day

18 Saturday

19 Sunday

Data provided 'as is' without warranty

20 Monday

21 Tuesday

22 Wednesday

Data provided 'as is' without warranty

March 2017

23 Thursday

24 Friday

25 Saturday — Maryland Day

26 Sunday — Prince Jonah Kuhio Kalanianaole Day

Data provided 'as is' without warranty

27 Monday Seward's Day

28 Tuesday

29 Wednesday

Data provided 'as is' without warranty

April 2017

30 Thursday

31 Friday César Chávez Day

01 Saturday

02 Sunday Pascua Florida Day

Data provided 'as is' without warranty

03 Monday

04 Tuesday

05 Wednesday

Data provided 'as is' without warranty

April 2017

06 Thursday

07 Friday

08 Saturday

09 Sunday

Data provided 'as is' without warranty

10 Monday

11 Tuesday

12 Wednesday

Data provided 'as is' without warranty

April 2017

13 Thursday

14 Friday

15 Saturday

16 Sunday

Data provided 'as is' without warranty

17 Monday	Patriot's Day

18 Tuesday

19 Wednesday

Data provided 'as is' without warranty

April 2017

20 Thursday

21 Friday San Jacinto Day

22 Saturday

23 Sunday

Data provided 'as is' without warranty

24 Monday

25 Tuesday

26 Wednesday

Data provided 'as is' without warranty

May 2017

27 Thursday

28 Friday

29 Saturday

30 Sunday

Data provided 'as is' without warranty

01 Monday

02 Tuesday

03 Wednesday

Data provided 'as is' without warranty

May 2017

04 Thursday — Independence Day (Rhode Island)

05 Friday

06 Saturday

07 Sunday

Data provided 'as is' without warranty

08 Monday	Truman Day

09 Tuesday

10 Wednesday

Data provided 'as is' without warranty

May 2017

11 Thursday

12 Friday

13 Saturday

14 Sunday

Data provided 'as is' without warranty

15 Monday

16 Tuesday

17 Wednesday

Data provided 'as is' without warranty

May 2017

18 Thursday

19 Friday

20 Saturday

21 Sunday

Data provided 'as is' without warranty

22 Monday

23 Tuesday

24 Wednesday

May 2017

25 Thursday

26 Friday

27 Saturday

28 Sunday

Data provided 'as is' without warranty

29 Monday	Memorial Day

30 Tuesday

31 Wednesday

Data provided 'as is' without warranty

June 2017

01 Thursday — Statehood Day (Kentucky, Tennessee)

02 Friday

03 Saturday

04 Sunday

Data provided 'as is' without warranty

05 Monday

06 Tuesday

07 Wednesday

Data provided 'as is' without warranty

June 2017

08 Thursday

09 Friday

10 Saturday

11 Sunday Kamehameha Day

Data provided 'as is' without warranty

12 Monday

13 Tuesday

14 Wednesday

June 2017

15 Thursday

16 Friday

17 Saturday Bunker Hill Day

18 Sunday

Data provided 'as is' without warranty

19 Monday

20 Tuesday West Virginia Day

21 Wednesday

Data provided 'as is' without warranty

June 2017

22 Thursday

23 Friday

24 Saturday

25 Sunday

Data provided 'as is' without warranty

26 Monday

27 Tuesday

28 Wednesday

Data provided 'as is' without warranty

July 2017

29 Thursday

30 Friday

01 Saturday

02 Sunday

Data provided 'as is' without warranty

03 Monday

04 Tuesday **Independence Day**

05 Wednesday

Data provided 'as is' without warranty

July 2017

06 Thursday

07 Friday

08 Saturday

09 Sunday

Data provided 'as is' without warranty

10 Monday

11 Tuesday

12 Wednesday

Data provided 'as is' without warranty

July 2017

13 Thursday

14 Friday

15 Saturday

16 Sunday

Data provided 'as is' without warranty

17 Monday

18 Tuesday

19 Wednesday

Data provided 'as is' without warranty

July 2017

20 Thursday

21 Friday

22 Saturday

23 Sunday

Data provided 'as is' without warranty

24 Monday Pioneer Day

25 Tuesday

26 Wednesday

Data provided 'as is' without warranty

July 2017

27 Thursday

28 Friday

29 Saturday

30 Sunday

Data provided 'as is' without warranty

31 Monday

01 Tuesday

02 Wednesday

Data provided 'as is' without warranty

August 2017

03 Thursday

04 Friday

05 Saturday

06 Sunday

Data provided 'as is' without warranty

07 Monday

08 Tuesday

09 Wednesday

August 2017

10 Thursday

11 Friday

12 Saturday

13 Sunday

Data provided 'as is' without warranty

14 Monday — Victory Day

15 Tuesday

16 Wednesday — Bennington Battle Day

Data provided 'as is' without warranty

August 2017

17 Thursday

18 Friday — Statehood Day (Hawaii)

19 Saturday

20 Sunday

Data provided 'as is' without warranty

21 Monday

22 Tuesday

23 Wednesday

August 2017

24 Thursday

25 Friday

26 Saturday

27 Sunday — Lyndon Baines Johnson Day

Data provided 'as is' without warranty

28 Monday

29 Tuesday

30 Wednesday

Data provided 'as is' without warranty

September 2017

31 Thursday

01 Friday

02 Saturday

03 Sunday

Data provided 'as is' without warranty

04 Monday	Labor Day

05 Tuesday

06 Wednesday

Data provided 'as is' without warranty

September 2017

07 Thursday

08 Friday

09 Saturday

10 Sunday

Data provided 'as is' without warranty

11 Monday

12 Tuesday

13 Wednesday

Data provided 'as is' without warranty

September 2017

14 Thursday

15 Friday

16 Saturday

17 Sunday

Data provided 'as is' without warranty

18 Monday

19 Tuesday

20 Wednesday

Data provided 'as is' without warranty

September 2017

21 Thursday

22 Friday

23 Saturday

24 Sunday

Data provided 'as is' without warranty

25 Monday

26 Tuesday

27 Wednesday

Data provided 'as is' without warranty

October 2017

28 Thursday

29 Friday

30 Saturday

01 Sunday

Data provided 'as is' without warranty

02 Monday

03 Tuesday

04 Wednesday

Data provided 'as is' without warranty

October 2017

05 Thursday

06 Friday

07 Saturday

08 Sunday

Data provided 'as is' without warranty

09 Monday **Columbus Day**

Indigenous People's Day

Native Americans' Day

10 Tuesday

11 Wednesday

Data provided 'as is' without warranty

October 2017

12 Thursday
13 Friday
14 Saturday
15 Sunday

Data provided 'as is' without warranty

16 Monday

17 Tuesday

18 Wednesday Alaska Day

Data provided 'as is' without warranty

October 2017

19 Thursday

20 Friday

21 Saturday

22 Sunday

Data provided 'as is' without warranty

23 Monday

24 Tuesday

25 Wednesday

Data provided 'as is' without warranty

October 2017

26 Thursday

27 Friday Nevada Day

28 Saturday

29 Sunday

Data provided 'as is' without warranty

30 Monday

31 Tuesday

01 Wednesday

Data provided 'as is' without warranty

November 2017

02 Thursday

03 Friday

04 Saturday

05 Sunday

Data provided 'as is' without warranty

06 Monday

07 Tuesday

08 Wednesday

Data provided 'as is' without warranty

November 2017

09 Thursday

10 Friday **Veterans Day**

11 Saturday

12 Sunday

Data provided 'as is' without warranty

13 Monday

14 Tuesday

15 Wednesday

Data provided 'as is' without warranty

November 2017

16 Thursday

17 Friday

18 Saturday

19 Sunday

Data provided 'as is' without warranty

20 Monday

21 Tuesday

22 Wednesday

Data provided 'as is' without warranty

November 2017

23 Thursday **Thanksgiving Day**

24 Friday Robert E Lee's Birthday (Georgia)

25 Saturday

26 Sunday

Data provided 'as is' without warranty

27 Monday

28 Tuesday

29 Wednesday

Data provided 'as is' without warranty

December 2017

30 Thursday

01 Friday

02 Saturday

03 Sunday

Data provided 'as is' without warranty

04 Monday
05 Tuesday
06 Wednesday

December 2017

07 Thursday

08 Friday

09 Saturday

10 Sunday

Data provided 'as is' without warranty

11 Monday

12 Tuesday

13 Wednesday

Data provided 'as is' without warranty

December 2017

14 Thursday

15 Friday

16 Saturday

17 Sunday

Data provided 'as is' without warranty

18 Monday

19 Tuesday

20 Wednesday

December 2017

21 Thursday

22 Friday

23 Saturday

24 Sunday

Data provided 'as is' without warranty

25 Monday	Christmas Day

26 Tuesday	Christmas Day

27 Wednesday

Data provided 'as is' without warranty

December 2017

28 Thursday

29 Friday

30 Saturday

31 Sunday

Data provided 'as is' without warranty

Federal Holidays 2017

DATE	DAY OF THE WEEK	HOLIDAY	REGION
January 1, 2017	Sunday	New Year's Day	Nationwide
January 13, 2017	Friday	Lee Jackson Day	Virginia
January 16, 2017	Monday	Martin Luther King Day	Nationwide
January 16, 2017	Monday	Idaho Human Rights Day	Idaho
January 16, 2017	Monday	Robert E Lee's Birthday	Alabama, Arkansas, Mississippi
January 19, 2017	Thursday	Robert E Lee's Birthday	Florida
January 29, 2017	Sunday	Kansas Day	
February 4, 2017	Saturday	Rosa Parks Day	California, Ohio
February 12, 2017	Sunday	Lincoln's Birthday	California, Connecticut, Missouri, Illinois
February 15, 2017	Wednesday	Susan B Anthony's Birthday	Florida
February 20, 2017	Monday	Washington's Birthday	Scotland
February 20, 2017	Monday	Presidents Day	Nationwide
March 2, 2017	Thursday	Texas Independence Day	Texas
March 6, 2017	Monday	Casimir Pulaski Day	Illinois
March 7, 2017	Tuesday	Town Meeting Day Vermont	Vermont
March 17, 2017	Friday	Evacuation Day	Massachusetts
March 25, 2017	Saturday	Maryland Day	Maryland
March 26, 2017	Sunday	Prince Jonah Kuhio Kalanianaole Day	Hawaii
March 27, 2017	Monday	Seward's Day	Alaska

Data provided 'as is' without warranty

Federal Holidays 2017

DATE	DAY OF THE WEEK	HOLIDAY	REGION
March 31, 2017	Friday	César Chávez Day	California, Colorado, Texas
April 2, 2017	Sunday	Pascua Florida Day	Florida
April 17, 2017	Monday	Patriot's Day	Massachusetts, Wisconsin, Main
April 21, 2017	Friday	San Jacinto Day	Texas
May 4, 2017	Thursday	Independence Day	Rhode Island
May 8, 2017	Monday	Truman Day	Missouri
May 29, 2017	Monday	Memorial Day	Nationwide
June 1, 2017	Thursday	Statehood Day	Kentucky, Tennessee
June 11, 2017	Sunday	Kamehameha Day	Hawaii
June 17, 2017	Samstag	Bunker Hill Day	Massachusetts
June 20, 2017	Tuesday	West Virginia Day	West Virginia
July 4, 2017	Tuesday	Independence Day	Nationwide
July 24, 2017	Monday	Pioneer Day	Utah
August 14, 2017	Monday	Victory Day	Rhode Island
August 16, 2017	Wednesday	Bennington Battle Day	Vermont
August 18, 2017	Friday	Statehood Day	Hawaii
August 27, 2017	Sunday	Lyndon Baines Johnson Day	Alaska
September 4, 2017	Monday	Labor Day	Nationwide
October 09, 2017	Monday	Columbus Day	Nationwide
October 09, 2017	Monday	Indigenous People's Day	California
October 09, 2017	Monday	Native Americans' Day	South Dakota
October 18, 2017	Wednesday	Alaska Day	Alaska
October 27, 2017	Friday	Nevada Day	Nevada
November 10, 2017	Friday	Veterans Day	Nationwide

Data provided 'as is' without warranty

Federal Holidays 2017

DATE	DAY OF THE WEEK	HOLIDAY	REGION
November 23, 2017	Thursday	Thanksgiving Day	Nationwide
November 24, 2017	Friday	Robert E Lee's Birthday	Georgia
December 25, 2017	Monday	Christmas Day	Nationwide
December 26, 2017	Tuesday	Christmas Day	Nationwide

Data provided 'as is' without warranty

Notes

Notes

Notes

Notes

Notes

Notes

Notes

Notes

Notes

Notes

Birthday Calendar

January	February	March	April	May	June
1	1	1	1	1	1
2	2	2	2	2	2
3	3	3	3	3	3
4	4	4	4	4	4
5	5	5	5	5	5
6	6	6	6	6	6
7	7	7	7	7	7
8	8	8	8	8	8
9	9	9	9	9	9
10	10	10	10	10	10
11	11	11	11	11	11
12	12	12	12	12	12
13	13	13	13	13	13
14	14	14	14	14	14
15	15	15	15	15	15
16	16	16	16	16	16
17	17	17	17	17	17
18	18	18	18	18	18
19	19	19	19	19	19
20	20	20	20	20	20
21	21	21	21	21	21
22	22	22	22	22	22
23	23	23	23	23	23
24	24	24	24	24	24
25	25	25	25	25	25
26	26	26	26	26	26
27	27	27	27	27	27
28	28	28	28	28	28
29	29	29	29	29	29
30		30	30	30	30
31		31		31	

Birthday Calendar

July	August	September	October	November	December
1	1	1	1	1	1
2	2	2	2	2	2
3	3	3	3	3	3
4	4	4	4	4	4
5	5	5	5	5	5
6	6	6	6	6	6
7	7	7	7	7	7
8	8	8	8	8	8
9	9	9	9	9	9
10	10	10	10	10	10
11	11	11	11	11	11
12	12	12	12	12	12
13	13	13	13	13	13
14	14	14	14	14	14
15	15	15	15	15	15
16	16	16	16	16	16
17	17	17	17	17	17
18	18	18	18	18	18
19	19	19	19	19	19
20	20	20	20	20	20
21	21	21	21	21	21
22	22	22	22	22	22
23	23	23	23	23	23
24	24	24	24	24	24
25	25	25	25	25	25
26	26	26	26	26	26
27	27	27	27	27	27
28	28	28	28	28	28
29	29	29	29	29	29
30	30	30	30	30	30
31	31		31		31

IMPRINT:

M. Woll

Eschweilerstraße 106

52477 Alsdorf

(GERMANY)

Made in the USA
Middletown, DE
10 November 2022

14569513R00071